SECOND LANGUAGE

SECOND LANGUAGE

Poems by
**LISEL
MUELLER**

Louisiana State University Press
Baton Rouge and London
1986

Designer: Christopher Wilcox
Typeface: Times Roman
Typesetter: G & S Typesetters
Printer: Thomson-Shore, Inc.
Binder: John Dekker & Sons, Inc.

Grateful acknowledgment is made to the editors of the following
publications, in which some of the poems herein first appeared:

*American Poetry Review, Atlantic, Black Warrior Review, Brockport
Forum, Clockwatch, Chicago Review, Georgia Review, Indiana Review,
Iowa Review, Midwest Poetry Review, Missouri Review, New England
Review/Breadloaf Quarterly, New Letters, Ohio Review, Overtures,
Oyez Review, Ploughshares, Paris Review, Poetry, Poetry Northwest,
raccoon, Tendril, TriQuarterly, Voices from the Forest, Willow Springs,
Woman Poet* (an anthology).

Library of Congress Cataloging-in-Publication Data

Mueller, Lisel.
  Second language.
  I. Title.
PS3563.U35S4   1986   811'.54   86-7246
ISBN 0-8071-1336-0
ISBN 0-8071-1337-9 (pbk.)

The present intrudes upon remembrance, today becomes the last day of the past. Yet we would suffer continuous estrangement from ourselves if it weren't for memory of the things we have done, of the things that have happened to us. If it weren't for the memory of ourselves.

—CHRISTA WOLF

CONTENTS

SECOND LANGUAGE

NECESSITIES

1.

A map of the world. Not the one in the atlas,
but the one in our heads, the one we keep coloring in.
With the blue thread of the river by which we grew up.
The green smear of the woods we first made love in.
The yellow city we thought was our future.
The red highways not traveled, the green ones
with their missed exits, the black side roads
which took us where we had not meant to go.
The high peaks, recorded by relatives,
though we prefer certain unmarked elevations,
the private alps no one knows we have climbed.
The careful boundaries we draw and erase.
And always, around the edges,
the opaque wash of blue, concealing
the dropoff they have stepped into before us,
singly, mapless, not looking back.

2.

The illusion of progress. Imagine our lives without it:
tape measures rolled back, yardsticks chopped off.
Wheels turning but going nowhere.
Paintings flat, with no vanishing point.
The plots of all novels circular;
page numbers reversing themselves past the middle.
The mountain top no longer a goal,
merely the point between ascent and descent.
All streets looping back on themselves;
life as a beckoning road an absurd idea.
Our children refusing to grow out of their childhoods;
the years refusing to drag themselves
toward the new century.
And hope, the puppy that bounds ahead,
no longer a household animal.

3.

Answers to questions, an endless supply.
New ones that startle, old ones that reassure us.

1

All of them wrong perhaps, but for the moment
solutions, like kisses or surgery.
Rising inflections countered by level voices,
words beginning with *w* hushed
by declarative sentences. The small, bold sphere
of the period chasing after the hook,
the doubter that walks on water
and treads air and refuses to go away.

4.

Evidence that we matter. The crash of the plane
which, at the last moment, we did not take.
The involuntary turn of the head,
which caused the bullet to miss us.
The obscene caller who wakes us at midnight
to the smell of gas. The moon's
full blessing when we fell in love,
its black mood when it was all over.
Confirm us, we say to the world,
with your weather, your gifts, your warnings,
your ringing telephones, your long, bleak silences.

5.

Even now, *the old things first things,*
which taught us language. Things of day and of night.
Irrational lightning, fickle clouds, the incorruptible moon.
Fire as revolution, grass as the heir
to all revolutions. Snow
as the alphabet of the dead, subtle, undeciphered.
The river as what we wish it to be.
Trees in their humanness, animals in their otherness.
Summits. Chasms. Clearings.
And stars, which gave us the word distance,
so we could name our deepest sadness.

I

VOYAGER

For my father, 1897–1976

No one's body could be that light,
not even after it burns—
I know this is not you,
has nothing to do with you

I know you stand on a ship
looking through the eyeholes
near-sighted and patient as always,
still knowing everything

No matter what language they speak,
the boatmen in the black barges
that pass you, you will answer

No matter what bundle of time
they inhabit, you will direct them,
warn them once more and once more in vain

You who changed countries more often than shoes
can step ashore anywhere;
loneliness is the anchor
you've always carried with you

                    *

The desert is what I would have spared you,
the wilderness after my mother died,
your fixed star

Everything could be borne,
all knowledge, all separation
except that final one

Slowly you turned to stone

And I, your daughter/keeper—
what did I know about
the sentience of stone?
I watered you with indignities
and tears, but you never bloomed

Now both of you have entered
the history of your photographs;
together, young and smiling,
you stand on the steps of Notre Dame

"These are my parents, friends and children,"
I say, but it is hopeless

I want the impossible photograph,
one that would show the world
your trick, how you and she
pulled joy from any borrowed hat
or sleeve, a survivor's art

This is the hardest knowledge:
that no one will remember you
when your daughters are gone

*

Five years before you died
I took your picture;
you were wearing a dark jacket
and your hair was white

Now I hold the negative
up to the light and the sun streams through
as though it were Notre Dame again,
the rose window

you are changed, you wear
the pale clothes of summer,
your skin and hair are black

How can you see, your glasses
are whitewashed and there are holes
where your teeth used to be

Nevertheless you smile at me
across an enormous distance
as you have so many times
to let me know you have arrived

BREAD AND APPLES

In the tale
the apple tree rises before her,
not in an orchard,
but solitary and sudden
in a world she does not know
is supernatural. It asks
in an old woman's voice
to be relieved of its red-faced burden.
Further on, in a field,
she hears the terrified cries
of bread almost burned in its fireplace.
She does not ask who made bread
in an uninhabited wilderness.

So memory raises landmarks,
unbidden, out of place
and time. My father sits
in the long-discarded chair;
the pages of the history book
he leafs through keep springing back
to the beginning. He does not explain
his presence here. Without a question
I pull the bread from the ashes
and place it on the ground to cool.

THE GARDEN

I bring my mother back to life,
her eyes still green, still laughing,
She is still not fashionably thin.

She looks past me
for the girl
she left her old age to.
She does not recognize her
in me, a graying woman
older than she will ever be.

How strange that in the garden
of memory where she lives
nothing ever changes;
the heavy fruit
cannot pull the branches
any closer to the ground.

BLOOD ORANGES

In 1936, a child
in Hitler's Germany,
what did I know about the war in Spain?
Andalusia was a tango
on a wind-up gramophone,
Franco a hero's face in the paper.
No one told me about a poet
for whose sake I might have learned Spanish
bleeding to death on a barren hill.
All I knew of Spain
were those precious imported treats
we splurged on for Christmas.
I remember pulling the sections apart,
lining them up, sucking each one
slowly, so the red sweetness
would last and last—
while I was reading a poem
by a long-dead German poet
in which the woods stood safe
under the moon's milky eye
and the white fog in the meadows
aspired to become lighter than air.

MIDNIGHT

The spirits are not fooled
by my faked sleep, my regular breathing;
the magic animations
do not take place. I wait
for the window to tear off its bandages,
cured of its blindness,
the tape recorder to fall in love
with its new blue voice,
the leggy shadows on the floor
to pick each other up and start dancing.
But only the photographs in my head
relent: tonight it is
my grandfather's small-boned figure
with its white mustache
standing on a boardwalk
in Europe, calling me back.
He waves as if it were easy,
as if it were now or never
that the sea between us
would part for my long walk home.

YOUR TIRED, YOUR POOR

Asylum

"I cannot ask you to paint the tops
of your bare mountains green
or gentle your coasts to lessen
my homesickness. Beggar, not chooser,
I hand you the life you say I must leave
at the border, bundled and tied.
You riffle through it without looking,
stamp it and put it out the back
for the trash collector. 'Next,' you call.

"I am free. I stand in the desert,
heavy with what I smuggled in
behind my eyes and under my tongue:
memory and language, my rod and staff,
my leper's rattle, my yellow star."

English as a Second Language

The underpaid young teacher
prints the letters *t, r, e, e*
on the blackboard and imagines
forests and gardens springing up
in the tired heads of her students.

But they see only four letters:
a vertical beam weighed down
by a crushing crossbar
and followed by a hook,
and after the hook, two squiggles,
arcane identical twins
which could be spying eyes
or ready fists, could be handles,
could be curled seedlings, could take root,
could develop leaves.

Crossing Over

There comes a day when the trees
refuse to let you pass
until you name them. Stones

speak up and reveal themselves
as the poor of your new country.
Then you see that the moon
has chosen to follow you here
and find yourself humming the music
you stuffed your ears against.
You dream in rhyme, in a language
you never wanted to understand.
When you pick up the telephone,
the voices from home arrive
sighing, bent by the ocean.
Their letters bear postage stamps
that surprise you with their strange, bright birds.

IDENTICAL TWINS

When they walk past me in the park
I shiver, as if two black cats
had crossed my path. Uncanny,
as if I were seeing things.
As if I were seeing two of me,
myself and the one in the mirror,
who must also be the one
I talk to when I'm alone.
The one I call "you," who loves me
better than any lover.
It is as though these sisters,
who tie their shoes in the same double bows
and bite their fingernails
down to the same horizon
existed to expose
twinlessness as a sham,
to let us know they know
about our secret:
the lost, illicit other
kept under lock and key
in the last room of the mind.

These days, riding the subway
to work and back, I notice
that the passengers move their lips
ever so slightly. I watch them
lean into themselves
as if toward a voice,
and then turn to the window
to search the backlit face
in the black, speeding mirror.

SOUTHPAW

Were you an only child? she asks.
No, but you've always favored the dreamer,
the star pitcher who writes novels,
the prophet with the red armband,
the low notes of the piano,
the swimmer against the stream.

You learned the truth early, that handles
are on the other side,
that doors are hinged to slow your entrance
and gloves and gadgets are made for others,
but you know that the ancient tools—
jugs, spoons, hammers, rakes—
care only about your opposable thumb.

It's your birthright, the extra effort
you've secretly come to love.
Left, left, the drill sergeant stutters,
and you smile like one of the chosen.
You push the reluctant ballpoint
forward, while the letters wave back,
and taste the word *sinister* on your tongue.
How enchanting it is, so sensuous,
the song of a mermaid with two left arms.

SECOND SIGHT

How cruel to have the future stuffed in one's eyes.
I think of a woman who shuns our extended hands
because she knows lifeline and heartline run off the palm
and come to a bad end in a place we can't see.
She must wish herself blind when she looks through our skins
at our deaths, at each particular death.
What is a flower to her except fallen petals?
The evening news tells her nothing;
her father's confident plans make her weep.
Revealing the grave near a country road
may lead to justice, but not joy,
though finding a hidden clearwater spring
should make her happy. Fall is her season;
while we rake leaves and smell snow in the air,
she smells lilacs and touches forsythia,
observes how the close-set redbud blossoms
run like a rash all the way down the branch.
Such are her short-lived reprieves from disasters
she sees but cannot prevent. How she must envy
our sightlessness, our ignorant eyes full of hope.

AFTER WHISTLER

There are girls who should have been swans.
At birth their feathers are burned;
their human skins never fit.
When the other children
line up on the side of the sun,
they will choose the moon,
that precious aberration.
They are the daughters mothers
worry about. All summer,
dressed in gauze, they flicker
inside the shaded house,
drawn to the mirror, where their eyes,
two languid moths, hang dreaming.
It's winter they wait for, the first snowfall
with the steady interior hum
only they can hear;
they stretch their arms, as if they were wounded,
toward the bandages of snow.
Briefly, the world is theirs
in its perfect frailty.

THE QUESTIONING

Mute and dazed, she has surfaced
in Memphis, Tennessee.
A squad car brought her in
just before dawn, before the sun
could turn its searchlight on her
and make her run. Fourteen,
perhaps fifteen, they think.
When they ask her about the cigarette burns
on her arms and ankles, she shakes her head.
She will not betray her keeper,
nor the location of hell.
When they offer her food, she suspects a trick.
For months or years she waited
for the rescue that did not come,
heard their feet overhead
coming and always going.
By now she denies them even her name.

No mother comes to claim her
and her emergence among us
does not explain the seasons.
It happens in autumn as well as spring;
it is happening now, somewhere
somebody's daughter comes stumbling
into the light, refusing
to give up her dark burden,
which is all she has brought from home.

"FROM DISCO QUEEN
TO GOSPEL PREACHER"

Beautiful Cindy chants
her shameful history
as if it were glory. Her talking arms
pull in the catcalls like applause.
She plays to their glittering eyes,
daring them to lay hands on her.

She knows they love her,
the hecklers and scoffers,
love her style, the way
she hefts the word *sin*
and teases them with the four soft strokes
of *for-ni-ca-tion,*
tempts them with the story
of how she tempted
the man in black beside her.

Expert, she gives herself
to the tense, dangerous thrill
of a woman stripping
before an audience of men,
and pulls back just in time,
suddenly sexless
under her cowboy shirt,
the brown skirt down to her feet.

FACE-LIFT

The woman who used to be my age
is shopping for endive and bell-shaped peppers.
Her face has retracted sleepless nights,
denies any knowledge of pain.
The black eyes given her
by the death of someone she loved
are gone. I look at her
wondering how it feels to remember,
under the skin of a thirty-year-old,
something that happened at forty.
I wonder if she excites her husband
in her new half-strangeness
or has betrayed him, removed
their years together like the soiled
part of a roller towel
yanked in the wrong direction.
Her unused face reveals nothing.
She moves ahead, her cart
piled high with greens, and reaches
for a bunch of jonquils, this year's first
yellow, about to open.

WIDOW

What the neighbors bring to her kitchen
is food for the living. She wants to eat
the food of the dead, their pure
narcotic of dry, black seeds.
Why, without him, should she desire
the endurance offered by meat and grain,
the sugars that glue the soul to the body?
She thanks them, but does not eat,
consumes strong coffee as if it were air
and she the vigilant candle
on a famous grave, until the familiar
sounds of the house become strange,
turn into messages in the new language
he has been forced to learn.
All night she works on the code,
almost happy, her body rising
like bread, while the food in its china caskets
dries out on the kitchen table.

THE EXHIBIT

My uncle in East Germany
points to the unicorn in the painting
and explains it is now extinct.
We correct him, say such a creature
never existed. He does not argue,
but we know he does not believe us.
He is certain power and gentleness
must have gone hand in hand
once. A prisoner of war
even after the war was over,
my uncle needs to believe in something
that could not be captured except by love,
whose single luminous horn
redeemed the murderous forest
and, dipped into foul water,
would turn it pure. This world,
this terrible world we live in,
is not the only possible one,
his eighty-year-old eyes insist,
dry wells that fill so easily now.

ABOUT SUFFERING
THEY WERE NEVER WRONG

They could have told us that the particulars,
those tiny chips, would remain embedded
in the mind she took with her,
the woman down the block
who hanged herself,

and that her mind was not like her house
with its open door, its yard full of flowers,

that even the cleanest floor
does not hide the absolute dropoff,
and when we walked past her windows,
thinking we looked into a room,
we looked at smoked glass and our own reflection.

How well they understood
that the lives of other people
are as full of secrets
as the lives of spies
who give up the trivial ones
to appease the neighbors,

and that the real one
implodes one sunny afternoon
in October, a day so mild
the roses are tricked into blooming again.

BEFORE THE CREDITS APPEAR
ON THE SCREEN

How smoothly the Greyhound takes
the curves around the mountains,
where trees have grouped themselves,
young and old together,
as if for a parade.

How cleanly the yellow line
divides the Interstate
into coming and going,
the cars rolling
perfectly distanced,
so reasonable you'd swear
some wild-eyed stranger
drunk or mad, would survive
if he stumbled into the road.

Believe, the music begs.
Believe in orderly lives:
milk poured, appointments kept,
beds settling nightly
into familiar shapes.
Believe in the unbruised highway,
the bus that takes curves like a skater,
the silver hounds at its sides
racing toward a town
where it is always summer.

And you believe, until the bus
stops to let someone on or off
and his particular story,
lonely and brutal, begins
with the dark letters of his name.

FIVE FOR COUNTRY MUSIC

I.   Insomnia

The bulb at the front door burns and burns.
If it were a white rose it would tire of blooming
through another endless night.

The moon knows the routine;
it beats the bushes from east to west
and sets empty-handed. Again the one
she is waiting for has outrun the moon.

II.   Old Money

The spotted hands shake as they polish the coins.

The shiny penny goes under the tongue,
the two silver pieces
weighted by pyramids
will shut down the eyes.

All the rest is paper,
useless in any world but this.

III.   Home Movie

She knows that walk, that whistle, that knock.

It's the black wolf who sticks
his floured paw underneath the door.

She tries not to open. One look at his face
and she'll drop the gun. He will pick it up
and turn it on her where she waits,
her eyes shining, her hands over her head.

IV.   Golden Boy

Whitewashed, the eyes refuse you.

And so the mouth must be serene,
the muscles play, the body
take an easy stance

to divert you from the two
boarded-up chambers
where someone has died.

V.   Washing Day

Each year her laundry line gets lighter.
One by one they disappear,
ten little Indians. They take their socks,
their jeans, their stiff plaid shirts.

Above the Ford on its concrete blocks,
striped and zippered,
her cotton dress flutters on and on.

LETTER TO CALIFORNIA

We write to each other as if
we were using the same language,
though we are not. Your sentences lap
over each other like the waves
of the Pacific, strictureless;
your long, sleek-voweled words
fill my mouth like ripe avocados.
To read you is to dismiss
news of earthquakes and mudslides,
to imagine time in slow motion.
It is to think of the sun
as a creature that will not let anything
happen to you.
                    Back here
we grow leeks and beans and sturdy
roots that will keep for months.
We have few disasters; i.e.,
no grandeur to speak of. Instead
we engage in a low-keyed continuous struggle
to get through the winter, which swallows
two seasons and throws its shadow
over a third. How do you manage
without snow to tell you that you are mortal?
We are brought up short by a wind
that shapes our words; they fall
in clean, blunt strokes. The birds here
are mostly chickadees
and juncos, monochromes
bred to the long view
like the sky under siege of lead
and the bony trees, which hold
the dancer's first position
month after month. But we have
our intimations: now and then
a cardinal with its lyric call,
its body blazing like a saint's
unexpectedly gaudy heart,

spills on our reasonable scene
of brown and gray, unconscious of itself.
I search the language for a word
to tell you how red is red.

METAPHOR

For Gregory Orr, who asked, "How can one teach
'Spring and Fall: To a Young Child' in the Hawaiian Islands?"

Your question persists, like the scent
of ginger blossoms, like the remembered
banyan trees whose aerated roots
seize the earth like the claws of a cast-out god.
How, in a place where *winter* means
a token lessening, an almost unnoticed
handicap on profusion,
like quiet stages inside our bodies,
which mean adjustment but not death,
not even simulation of death.
Not like snow, the old metaphor
for the bleached shroud; not like the trees
outside my window, all bare bones,
those terrible reminders
which also comfort in their mute
indifference. Yesterday
it was 80° in Honolulu,
while here in the frozen grass
a hungry owl dug its claws
into a rabbit in broad daylight.
But that's taxonomy; change the names
and you have a tropical bird and its prey.
No difference there. And perhaps
the shock and clatter of loosening leaves
is greater in the imagination
of those who live in paradise
than it is for us who see it happen,
just as we dream the plumage
of equinoctial parrots
even gaudier than it is,
and a deaf-blind child
imagined a Venice so splendid
she could not sleep all night.

Perhaps today a girl
who might have been your student
is driving around the island
changed. Someone she loved has died.

She stares at the prodigal trees,
the bold, insistent flowers,
but all she sees is a bitter landscape:
goldengrove unleaving,
bare ruin'd choirs, where late the sweet birds sang.

STORM

To see the lightning
as a question mark
made by a trembling hand

and hear the thunder
as its dreaded answer,
ambiguous in the distance
but, close, a rebuke as brutal
as a clean blow to the head—

such childish superstition
comes back to you at night
when you lie still, enduring
the bludgeoning of the fissured dark,
still powerless, still guilty.

MUSHROOMS

Only the dead could be
more ignorant of green
than these pale aliens,
sleepwalkers so strange
to the privilege of light
they refuse to turn up their faces,
keeping everything hidden
in the tight folds of their mantles.
Overnight they have turned
our yard into a burial ground
whose neglected, sunken markers
they are. We walk among them
like visitors and wonder
why here, these hooded deputies
with roots so tentative
they could have settled anywhere.

FACETS

When you look at a bee,
give it your simple-eyed
appraisal of intention,
hundreds of eyes look back.
One lights on the childhood scar
under your lip, one counts
the pulse in your temple, one
discovers the rip in your blouse—
but why go on? You are
segmented, a Cubist figure,
and you stand, the only actor,
in an amphitheater
of purple clover, watched
by thousands who miss nothing,
who catch the slightest flicker
of an eyelash, a hair on your arm.
You will never be
the innocent you were
before you read about them,
their habits, and how ancient,
almost eternal, they are.
There was a time when you put ice
on an occasional bee sting
and then forgot it, thinking
it inadvertent, haphazard,
that nothing would kill itself over you.

MILKWEED PODS IN WINTER

Two months in the house
have steamed them open:
wide, curved mouths
brimful of feathers,
as if speech had been held back
and wanted out, to fly
like those white surprises,
our briefly visible words,
when we speak in the frozen air.

If this is speech, it is
the speech of silence, winter speech.
It is what we would say to each other
if we could find the heart,
if there were no music
to say it for us
and the appetite of our bodies
did not swallow language clean.

We would be like these milkweed pods,
overflowing.

ACCOMMODATIONS

The house painter is not sentimental
and sets the wasps' nest on fire,
and the tribe of wasps is not proud
or dissuadable, and soon
a new nest hangs overhead.
We walk in and out of the door
under their home, a sponge
with oversized holes, quite safe,
keeping our downstairs distance
from their upstairs goings-on.

We're busy chasing a squirrel
which terrorizes our undersized
black and white cat, whose heart
pummels all parts of her body,
demanding an out, until she falls
on the red terrace. I want to poison
the squirrel, but of course I don't,
and the cat recovers and looks with desire
at the aspens which have grown so tall—

up from the scarred old bark
near the ground, to the milky skin
with its irregular love-bites
above, where the birds keep climbing
nearer and nearer the sun,
our ancient, hovering nurse,
scatterbrained but intact
and close enough for comfort.

FOR THE STRANGERS

Even this late in the century
it's hard to think of them
as simply creatures with feathered caps
and matchstick bones arranged into wings,
a species that never carried
our secrets in their gravelly craws
or under their downy shoulders
and, though their eyes are glazed,
never flew high enough
to share the altitude of the dead.

Of course we've known for a long time
that no painted god of the sun
or lover gone south received our message,
the one we never could find
the exact words for,
that it was a mistake
to confuse our perpetual hunger
for distance with their nature.

Keats knew it too, when he took his grief
to the deaf but convenient nightingale.
The fiction of metaphor saved us
from madness, perhaps from crime,
certainly from the despair
of admitting the broken connection,
that the world resists meaning
not to tease us, but because
there is no meaning
except the one we invent.

And where does that leave us now—
where does it leave me each October
when hundreds of blackbirds interrupt
their journey for a rest
in my backyard, when they could have chosen
to unsettle the neighbors
with their massive, ear-splitting presence?
I was born too late to believe in election.

When they return to the sky,
composing themselves in the ancient pen-strokes
that will carry them forward
into the twenty-first century,
I stand and stare at their far-flung
unreadable signature.
No intention, I tell myself,
this is no sign, but the habit
of homage persists, the upturned face,
the eyes glossed with astonishment.

UP NORTH

Already they are flying back,
gray clumps with nervous wings,
always the first to know.

Otherwise, mere inklings.
An occasional fiery branch
flags us down from the green,
but the leaves still rub soft-skinned
against each other, and the tomatoes
dawdle as though red
were a suitor willing to wait.
The trunks of the birches are lit
from within, like ideal nudes
who have no season. We lie
body to body under the trees
as we did last summer. Nothing has changed.
I search your face for the year,
but my eyes have aged at the same rate
and I've learned nothing. Plums
on the table beside us hoard
their juice inside sealed barrels
of gleaming skin, but you and I
don't hoard our sweetness, hoard anything.

SCENIC ROUTE

For Lucy, who called them "ghost houses."

Someone was always leaving
and never coming back.
The wooden houses wait like old wives
along this road; they are everywhere,
abandoned, leaning, turning gray.

Someone always traded
the lonely beauty
of hemlock and stony lakeshore
for survival, packed up his life
and drove off to the city.
In the yards the apple trees
keep hanging on, but the fruit
grows smaller year by year.

When we come this way again
the trees will have gone wild,
the houses collapsed, not even worth
the human act of breaking in.
Fields will have taken over.

What we will recognize
is the wind, the same fierce wind,
which has no history.

REASONS FOR NUMBERS

1

Because I exist

2

Because there must be a reason
why I should cast a shadow

3

So that good can try to be better
and become best
and beginning grow into middle and end

4

So the round earth can have its corners
and the house will not fall down around me

So the seasons will go on holding hands
and the string quartet play forever

5

For the invention of Milton and Shakespeare
and the older invention
of the wild rose, mother
to the petals
of my hand

6

Because
five
senses
are
not
enough

7

Because luck
is always odd

and the division
of history
into lean and fat

            years
mysterious

8

To make the spider
possible
and the black ball which tells me
the game is up

but also to let
the noise of the world
make itself heard
as music

9

For the orbit of Jupiter
            Saturn
            Venus
            Mars
            Mercury
            Uranus
            Mickey Mantle
            Lou Gehrig
            Babe Ruth

10

Created functionless, for the sheer play
of the mind in its tens of thousands of moves

There is nothing like it in nature

STALKING THE POEM

I.

Only one word will do. It isn't on the tip of your tongue, but you know it's not far. It's the one fish that won't swim into your net, a figure that hides in a crowd of similar figures, a domino stone in the face-down pool. Your need to find it becomes an obsession, singleminded and relentless as lust. It's a long time before you can free yourself, let it go. "Forget it," you say, and think that you do. When the word is sure you have forgotten it, it comes out of hiding. But it isn't taking any chances even now and has prepared its appearance with care. It surrounds itself with new and inconspicuous friends and faces you in a showup line in which everyone looks equally innocent. Of course you know it instantly, the way Joan of Arc knew the Dauphin and Augustine knew God. You haven't been so happy in weeks. You rush the word to your poem, which had died for lack of it, and it arises pink-cheeked as Lazarus. The two of you share the wine.

II.

You've got the poem cornered. It gives up, lies down, plays dead. No more resistance. How easily you could take it into your teeth and walk off with it! But you are afraid of the sound they will make crunching the bones. You are afraid of the taste of blood, of the poem's dark, unknown insides. So you stand above it, sniffing its fur, poking and pushing it, turning it over. Suddenly you see that its eyes are open and that they stare at you with contempt. You walk away with your tail between your legs. When you return the poem has disappeared.

III.

The poem is complete in your head, its long, lovely shape black against the white space in your mind. Each line is there, secure, recallable, pulled forth by the line before it and the one before that, like a melody whose second part you can sing once you have sung the first, but not before. All there, all perfectly linked. But when you pick up the pen, the shape dissolves, pales, spreads into slovenliness. You feel the poem escaping; you can't write fast enough. By some miracle you recover all the bits and pieces, and you manage to put them in their proper order. You have been saved, you think. But the poem is not the beautiful figure you held in your mind. It is gawky and gaptoothed; its arms are too long for its body; its clothes don't fit. It looks up at you from the page accusingly. "Look at the mess you've made," it says. "See what you can do with me. Last chance. Don't blow it." Filled with gratitude, you roll up your sleeves and go to work.

BLUE

Even the heart, with its pretensions to red,
is indigo; nor do silver
and raspberry skies deceive us
for long. No matter how murky
the river, a child's blue crayon
will restore it, perhaps a child
who has never seen a river.
If the imagination
were interior space,
its walls would be blue, a deep
shade like the alpine gentian
a climber risks his life for,
or the feathered iridescence
that does not know why your hand trembles
when you enter its name
into a record of astonishing events.

Your hand—
and when you turn it
palm upward, there are the veins
threaded through your wrist.
Such fragile stems.
And such a strong declaration
against the needle and the razor blade.

FENESTRATION

The surgeon says he will cut
a window in your ear
and you will hear again.

He tells you sound is light;
he will break through the convent wall
and give you back
music as figure and shadow,
the chiaroscuro of words.

Once more you will wave to a voice
until it has dropped behind the hill.

WORK TO BE DONE

For Ardyth Bradley

1.

Whatever happens, I was once
a creature of the water,
changing from minnow to newt
and emerging green and golden,
a turtle climbing ashore
to walk under leaves, in the broken
footprints of the sun.
My hands, my pair of fossils,
tell me that much. Water has etched
rills and gorges into my palms,
furrows that are supposed to reveal
my years, my chance for happiness,
the secret flaw that will kill me.
I can't decipher the code,
I only see twin cousins
to crab and barnacle
and read with increasing wonder
how far I have come.

2.

A man has designed a pair
of mechanical steel hands
to lift enormous weights
and place them precisely. It works
up to a point. At that point
human hands with their perfect pitch
must come into play, tiny muscles,
nerves assaulted by stimuli
like gifted children, living hands—
mine, turned into Lewis and Clark
in the shrubbery of your hair,
on the trail around your ear,
drifting like Père Marquette
down your long, cool arms,
falling asleep half-open
as common roses do.

3.

My nuns, my pair of moles,
life shows up in its costume of terror,
and what do you do but see
that I survive. With my mind
at gunpoint down a hole,
my feet bound together,
my voice stuffed in its box,
you continue to turn on lights,
set food on the table,
bring in the mail, pay bills,
pick up something fallen,
accurate as bats.

4.

No, my hands, you are nothing
like updated angel wings;
you are not doves, nor loaves
of snow; forget your dreams.
You are rough and full of bumps,
your fingers are short and stubby—
but listen, my useful sisters,
my down-to-earth redeemers,
my spoons, my hooks and wrenches,
my feelers, my two mimes;
do not become arthritic,
do not get caught in a door,
stay on good terms with saws,
stay away from fires,
stay with me.

STONE SOUP

So easy to stir up a feast
with only a random, unmagical stone
or, in some versions, the nail
we happen to carry around in our pockets.
It takes nothing more than hope
and, being persuaded, our natural gift
for persuasion to bring out the neighbors
with carrots and onions and parsley
and finally even meat and salt.
We stand in front of a window
behind which a nurse lifts you up,
newborn. We are holding
the ingredients for your future.
Already you have been given a name,
a second skin, more durable than the first.
Now your father is adding his vision
of you in twelve years, your beauty,
a long-term stowaway, hinted at;
your grandmother offers her trust
in your resilience, your aunt her assumption
of your genius for love.
And you, our odd-shaped, sea-worn stone,
our gleaming, crooked nail,
you let it happen, let the savor
of your life begin to simmer.

FULFILLING THE PROMISE

1.

A man I know named Booker
runs a secondhand bookstore.
My florist's name is Fiore.
Formica designs kitchens
in California, and Richard Hazard
sells real estate and insurance.
We can change our names
or grow into them.

2.

Except the unlucky ones.
Even their murderers knew
the children of the Czar
were innocent. But they could not kill
the name Romanoff
without killing its bearers.

3.

Today, in the hospital nursery,
I visit Grace, asleep
under a pink blanket,
her hands still curled into shells.
She lies between Tiffany
and Marvella, who soon must wear
the heavy crowns of their names.
Her mother named her Grace
in spite of her red skin
and her head like an egg. She likes
the old-fashioned sound. "Give her time
to fulfill the promise," she says.

4.

At her wedding, a woman gave up
half of her name
and exchanged it for another.
Half of her is public,
subject to trade; the other

private, treasure and loneliness,
what he thinks of as *her,*
what she would share, if she could.

5.

And the man who testified
for the State, who named the mobster,
how does he manage the old self
behind the new glasses
and the removable beard?
Under the memorized name
and the false documents
the container and spinner of memory
endures uninterrupted.
At night, with the lights out
and the TV turned up,
a woman whispers his secret name:
it frightens and excites him,
like the hundredth name of God.

STILL LIFE

Think of the time the words
in a book you had not read
for thirty years flew out
and stung you, fierce and sudden
in the plenitude of their truth,
or of the black piano,
a darkness that has no music
until it is touched and you are stunned
by your own desire.

So it is with this painting,
an arrangement of things. Even here,
where the fork points north forever,
it will stop gleaming
if you look long enough;
the moon in the goblet will sink,
the russet apple wrinkle;
and the snapdragon won't,
finally, hold its tongues—

red on red, they'll fall
in heaps on the blue cloth
which deepens under fire.

MONET REFUSES THE OPERATION

Doctor, you say there are no haloes
around the streetlights in Paris
and what I see is an aberration
caused by old age, an affliction.
I tell you it has taken me all my life
to arrive at the vision of gas lamps as angels,
to soften and blur and finally banish
the edges you regret I don't see,
to learn that the line I called the horizon
does not exist and sky and water,
so long apart, are the same state of being.
Fifty-four years before I could see
Rouen cathedral is built
of parallel shafts of sun,
and now you want to restore
my youthful errors: fixed
notions of top and bottom,
the illusion of three-dimensional space,
wisteria separate
from the bridge it covers.
What can I say to convince you
the Houses of Parliament dissolve
night after night to become
the fluid dream of the Thames?
I will not return to a universe
of objects that don't know each other,
as if islands were not the lost children
of one great continent. The world
is flux, and light becomes what it touches,
becomes water, lilies on water,
above and below water,
becomes lilac and mauve and yellow
and white and cerulean lamps,
small fists passing sunlight
so quickly to one another
that it would take long, streaming hair
inside my brush to catch it.
To paint the speed of light!
Our weighted shapes, these verticals,

burn to mix with air
and change our bones, skin, clothes
to gases. Doctor,
if only you could see
how heaven pulls earth into its arms
and how infinitely the heart expands
to claim this world, blue vapor without end.

V

A DAY LIKE ANY OTHER

Such insignificance: a glance
at your record on the doctor's desk
or a letter not meant for you.
How could you have known? It's not true
that your life passes before you
in rapid motion, but your watch
suddenly ticks like an amplified heart,
the hands freezing against a white
that is a judgment. Otherwise, nothing.
The face in the mirror is still yours.
Two men pass on the sidewalk
and do not stare at your window.
Your room is silent, the plants
locked inside their mysterious lives
as always. The queen-of-the-night
refuses to bloom, does not accept
your definition. It makes no sense,
your scanning the street for a traffic snarl,
a new crack in the pavement,
a flag at half-mast—signs
of some disturbance in the world,
some recognition that the sun
has turned its dark face toward you.

THE THOUSAND AND FIRST NIGHT

I did what the rug makers do:
begin at the edges, leave no gaps,
tie all loose ends, connect
everything. I have worked us
into the center, king and queen
enclosed by the fantastic hedge
of animals and plants
I invented to keep me alive.
My husband points to his newly
acquired heart, which shows
bright as glass through the skin
and beats as fast as a cuckoo's
against my cheek. O, the mercy
of language, whose spellbound figures
inhabit the walls of the mind
until the monster finally dreams
his human origins! Tonight
no one dies in this kingdom.

By morning I will have turned into
a character, stripped of foresight,
ignorant of connections,
in the only story I cannot invent.
A tale of horror perhaps,
bloody and short. It may cancel
all benign transformations.
I look at my husband the strangler's hands:
lunar, disarmed by sleep,
perfumed by my skin. I cannot imagine
how this story ends.

NEW YEAR'S

Outside the house a crow
has taken over the bare oak,
rises and falls at will
like a piece of soot from the chimney.
In another time zone
a colonel flaps his wings.
This first day of the year
is someone's ninety-first
in an underground prison cell
he cannot stand up in. At twilight
the winter trees reach out
with the graceless arms of the old,
or the not-yet-graceful
arms of young girls. What matters
is the gesture, the pure assertion
in the articulate wind.
It's not the trees I'm afraid for,
but the sky behind them,
that handblown mauve and pearl
left from a gentler century.
As if you could shatter it
with any common rock
and walk right into darkness.

CHANCES ARE

100 schoolchildren murdered by Bokassa I
    in Central African Empire
Uterus removed, New Zealand woman gives birth
    to healthy daughter
        —Two newspaper headlines on facing pages

Hope is a fat seed pod,
skin stretched tight around it,
ready to burst. When it does
the ancient crier calls
the light year of the child.

Every few seconds they arrive,
shot into time and space,
their mouths remembering
the shape of buds. In Ohio
a woman diminishing to a stalk
in a white bed picks up
the newspaper and reads
about one hundred children
massacred by their government.
Dismisses it. She skips
to a story she can believe
in the presence of her child's
soft, rhythmic tugs. She imagines
a magic country of sheep
at the bottom of the world,
where even barren women
give birth; a five-pound body
bearing the weight of the earth;
the breath that keeps it turning.

INTO SPACE

How light we are becoming.

Our diets of greens and seeds
hollow us, bring us closer
to the birds;
our buoyant winter coats
are stuffed for luck
with incipient feathers.

Everything in our lives
is thinning down, prepares itself
for the weightless future.

Lasers replace cumbersome tools,
boxes diminish to buttons;
soon our messy, erroneous hearts
will be superseded
and the gigantic god
of history dwarfed to a nylon tape
we carry in our pockets.

*

Like mountain climbers and athletes,
we undergo daily training

We go out in the morning
and when we return
our houses are thirty stories high,
our names not listed
in the lobby

We float to the top of the building,
naked in glass elevators,
and when we emerge our neighbors
meet us with guns, just in case

They look at us round-eyed
and ask who we are

Back on the street, our feet
lift off the ground, the trees
and lampposts we reach for back off
into the painted distance

*

In a recurrent dream
I am asked to step out of my shoes,
fold and stack my clothes,
place the contents of my purse
on a desk for later disposal.
I leave my daughter's photographed hands,
my other daughter's new poem,
my keys, my driver's license
with the bad picture, my Chinese
address book with its birds and flowers.
Strip-searched, I am forced to surrender
my mother's bookmark of dried heather
taped to the sole of my foot
and my husband's twenty-year-old face
in a heart-shaped locket concealed in my hair.
Finally, when I step on the scales
no lights flash;
the X-ray scanner sweeps over me
and finds me empty.

*

Think of the sac of memory
as the last resort,
the bundle the refugees tie to a stick
when they cross the frozen river

Think of the contents, volatile
as dandelion fluff
when we finally scatter it
into the atmosphere we are leaving

Think of it falling on someone
who suspects nothing,
who is suddenly moved to recall
a forgotten childhood scene
and finds himself stunned by its gravity.